CASTING
a VISION

The Past and Future of Spiritual Formation

—————

Richard J. Foster

Scripture quotations are from New Revised Standard Version Bible, copyright © 1989
National Council of the Churches of Christ in the United States of America. Used by
permission. All rights reserved worldwide.

"My little children, for whom I am again in the pain of childbirth until Christ is formed in you . . ."
– Galatians 4:19

In June of 2018, a number of Christian pastors and ministry leaders gathered at George Fox University for a three-day conference. During that time, we remembered with thanksgiving the strides that have been made in the last four decades since the publication of *Celebration of Discipline*. Even more importantly, we gathered to consider the best ways to faithfully minister to our people as they deal with the daily struggles and joys of life in this first half of the twenty-first century.

To mark the occasion of the fortieth anniversary of the publication of *Celebration of Discipline*, I was asked to attempt to cast a vision for the next forty years. Now any attempt to predict the future is risky business, so our efforts need to be undertaken with the utmost care and humility of heart. So we pray: *Dear Lord, enlarge our hearts and minds toward all those things that reflect the Trinitarian passion. Amen.*

Discovering a Theology of Spiritual Growth

Our world today cries out for a theology of spiritual growth that has been proven to work in the midst of the harsh realities of daily life. Sadly, many today have simply given up on the possibility of growth in character formation.

Vast numbers of well-intended folk have exhausted themselves in church work and discovered that these things did not substantively change the inner life. They found that they were just as impatient and egocentric and fearful as when they began lifting the heavy load of church work. Maybe more so.

Others have immersed themselves in multiple social-service projects. And while the glow of helping others lingers for a time, they soon realized that all their Herculean efforts left little lasting imprint on the inner life. Indeed, it often made them much worse inwardly—frustrated and angry and bitter.

Still others have a practical theology that simply will not allow for spiritual growth. Indeed, they just might see it as a bad thing. Having been saved by grace, these individuals have become paralyzed by it. For them, any attempt to make progress forward in the spiritual life smacks of "works righteousness." Since their liturgies tell them that they sin in word, thought, and deed daily, they have concluded that this is their fate until they die. Heaven is their only release from this world of sin and rebellion. Hence these folk—good folk, well-meaning folk—will sit in the pew year after year without a millimeter of movement forward in the spiritual life.

Finally, there is a general cultural malaise that touches us all to one extent or another. I am referring to how completely we have become accustomed to the normality of dysfunction. The constant stream of scandals and broken marriages and mayhem of every sort undermines our sensitivity to moral integrity.

Michael Gerson has observed that our culture is constantly shouting out to us, "Blessed are the proud. Blessed are the ruthless. Blessed are the shameless. Blessed are those who hunger and thirst after fame." This all-pervasive dysfunction in our culture today makes it nearly impossible for us to have a clear vision of spiritual progress under God. Shining models of wholeness and holiness are so rare today.

And yet echoing down through the centuries is a great company of witnesses telling us of a life vastly richer and deeper and fuller. In all human circumstances—good and bad and even tragic—they have found a life of "righteousness and peace and joy in the Holy Spirit" (Rom 14:17) to be actually possible. They have discovered that real, solid, substantive transformation into the likeness of Jesus Christ *is* realizable. They witness to a deep character transformation that is well-nigh amazing. They have seen their own sinful thoughts and egocentric passions give way to such a selflessness and humility of heart that it has astonished even them. Rage and hate and malice are replaced with love and compassion and universal goodwill.

There is a record of more than two thousand years of great ones in this life—Augustine and Francis and Teresa and à Kempis and Julian and many, many more. These were people who by following hard after Jesus became persons of absolute sterling character. The record is there for anyone who wants to see.

Incarnating a With-God Life into Daily Experience

Now our first task—our great task, our central task—is incarnating this reality of a with-God life into the daily experience of our people right where they live and work and cry and pray and curse the darkness. If we do not make substantial progress forward here, all our other efforts will simply dry up and blow away. The actual substance of our lives needs to be so dramatically different—transformed at the deepest subterranean level—that everyone can see the difference and glorify God, who has caused the difference.

But now, before we begin in earnest, it is critical for us to remind ourselves that spiritual formation is *not* a tool kit for "fixing" our culture or our churches or even our individual lives. "Fixing" things is simply not our business. So we stoutly refuse to use formation work in order to "save America from its moral decline," or to restore churches to their days of former glory, or even to rescue people from their destructive behaviors. Such forming, conforming, and transforming realities belong to God alone. Please understand—there is plenty for us to do in this work, but transforming the human heart is a divine prerogative.

We begin with growing the human person before God. God has given each one of us the responsibility to "grow in grace." You cannot do that for me and I cannot do that for you. We are to take up our own individualized cross and follow in the steps of the crucified and risen Christ.

All real formation effort is "heart work." And for good reason, for the heart is the wellspring of all human action. All the devotional masters call us constantly, repeatedly, almost monotonously, toward purity of heart. For example, the great Puritan divines gave sustained attention to this "heart work," as they called it. In *Keeping the Heart,* John Flavel, a seventeenth-century English Puritan, observed, "The greatest difficulty in conversion is to win the heart *to* God. The greatest difficulty after conversion is to keep the heart *with* God. . . .

Heart-work is hard work indeed."

Now in this "heart work," external actions are *not* the center of our concerns. Outward actions are wholly secondary—a natural result of something far deeper, far more profound.

The constant appeal of the devotional masters to heart purity is a profound word for you and me—"profound" because we have a perpetual tendency to neglect this most important, most central, most critical, "heart work." And the effects of this neglect are written across the face of humanity. So we continually cry out to God, "Search me, O God, and know my heart; test me and know my thoughts. See if there is any wicked way in me, and lead me in the way everlasting" (Ps 139:23–24).

You see, we are—each and every one of us—a tangled mass of motives: hope and fear, faith and doubt, simplicity and duplicity, honesty and falsehood, openness and guile. God knows our heart better than we can ever know our heart. God alone can separate the true from the false. God is the only one who can purify the motives of the heart.

The most important, the most real, the most lasting work is accomplished in the depths of our heart. This work is solitary and interior. It cannot be seen or fully understood by any human being, not even ourselves. It is a work known only to God. It is the work of heart purity, of soul conversion, of inward transformation, of life formation.

Let me attempt to describe what this process looks like. It begins by our quieting all "creaturely activity," as the old writers put it. We are to become still, even though everything around us feels dark.

James Nayler, a seventeenth-century Christian leader, counsels, "Art thou in the darkness? Well, mind it not, for if you mind it, it will feed thee more. But stand still and act not and wait in patience until the Light of Christ arises out of darkness to lead thee."

So we wait, yielded and still. And when Jesus, "the true light, which enlightens everyone" (Jn 1:9), comes to us, we turn toward the light of Christ. For some of us, this is an excruciatingly slow "turning, turning, till we come round right." For others of us, it is instantaneous and glorious. In either case, we are coming to trust in Jesus—to accept Jesus not just as our Savior but as our Life. We are born from above, as we read about in John 3.

But our being *born* from above, of necessity, includes our being *formed* from above. Being spiritually born is a beginning—a wonderful, glorious beginning. It is not an ending. The heart is cleansed, but it has yet to be purified. The work of the cross contains a "double cure," as the old hymn "Rock of Ages" puts it.

> Let the water and the blood,
> From Thy wounded side which flowed,
> Be of sin *the double cure,*
> Save from wrath and make me pure.

So often today we only speak of the first part of this work of the cross. We talk a lot about our being "saved from wrath."

(And this is indeed a wonderful reality, isn't it?) But as the hymn says, this work involves a "double cure." The salvation that is in Jesus Christ also aims to make us pure. You see, God's intent is to turn us into the kind of persons that can safely and easily reign with God.

So now we are ushered into this new ongoing, living relationship. As Peter puts it in his first letter, we "have been born anew, not of perishable but of imperishable seed, through the living and enduring word of God." God is real. Jesus is alive and active in our little affairs.

Now all real formation work has a local address. We undertake these efforts in the context of the community of faith. We pray together. We learn together. We laugh together. We weep together. We suffer together.

Throughout this formation process, our task as pastors is simply and profoundly to be *with* our people in this "heart work." Jesus Christ is the Good Shepherd, and we serve as under-shepherds. And as under-shepherds we are to have the smell of the sheep on us. So what do we do? We stand *with* our people. We pray *with* our people. We weep *with* our people. We laugh and sing and celebrate *with* our people. And we also ask the vexing, puzzling, heartrending questions *with* our people. We are there *with* our people regardless of the outcome, even if this involves no more than helping to pick up the pieces when the results are tragic.

Challenges We Face Today That Did Not Exist Forty Years Ago

Up to this point I have shared with you issues that were equally true forty years ago when I first penned *Celebration of Discipline*. The need for the growth of the soul was true then and it is true now.

It is now time for us to consider issues that present new challenges to our people today that did not exist forty years ago. I have four areas of concern here.

1. Our Technological Revolution

Perhaps the most obvious change from forty years ago is the explosion of information technologies in our day. Back when I wrote *Celebration*, the Internet was barely on the horizon. "Cookies" were for eating. "Having a virus" meant we were sick. Hackers were unheard of. But now we have computers we can hold in our hands or strap to our wrists.

This technological revolution is not unlike the explosion of information that was produced by Gutenberg and his movable type in the fifteenth century. The big difference between these two revolutions is that today the changes are coming at us with lightning speed.

And all this emailing and texting and tweeting have created one challenge that does indeed impinge upon the spiritual life. I can state this challenge in one word: *distraction*. Distraction is *the* primary spiritual problem in contemporary culture. Frankly, when we are perpetually distracted, we are unable to discern the *Kol Yahweh*, the voice of the Lord.

Oh for the day when all we had to do was turn off the TV if we wanted solitude and silence! Now we click through an endless stream of Internet links, read tweets from God knows who, check email constantly, text family and others, and mindlessly scroll through Facebook.

Even more insidious are the ways we are bombarded by the broad distractions of constant noise, constant demands, constant news. Everyone, it seems, wants us to be accessible 24/7 and to respond instantly to any and every request. If we delay answering an email for even an hour or two, people become worried that something is wrong with us. Neuroscience studies are now showing us that the neural pathways of our brains are being rewired accordingly, so that our physical capacity for sustained attention is decreasing.

We, of course, complain endlessly about our wired world. But—let's be honest—we do enjoy our technological gluttony.

So we need a discerning, life-giving technological asceticism. I work on these matters in my new foreword to the fortieth-anniversary edition of *Celebration*, so I'll let you read about it in the book. I did learn one thing this past week. If we will fast from food periodically it will help to temper the spirit of constantly grasping for control, and this will make it easier for us to fast from technology now and again.

2. *The Loss of a Christian Consciousness*

A second challenge I want us to think about is the loss of

a Christian consciousness in contemporary culture. To say it bluntly, church life—its story and its culture—is today lost to vast numbers of precious people. When I wrote *Celebration*, roughly 45 percent of the population attended church. I don't know what the statistic would be today, but it is clearly much less than it was forty years ago.

Now please understand me—I'm not so much concerned about getting church attendance higher as I am about how we can minister life to people today right where they are.

Do you remember the old parish system where a pastor or priest had responsibility for the spiritual welfare of everyone in that parish, regardless of whether they ever attended church or not? This is the paradigm I am thinking about.

Thomas Merton tells the story of the Russian spiritual director who spent a large amount of time talking with a lady in the village about her turkeys. When he was criticized for investing so much time and energy talking with this lady about something so trivial, he replied, "It's not trivial to her. To her these turkeys matter. Don't you understand? This woman's whole life is in those turkeys!"

Long ago, when I was pastoring in Oregon, I became acquainted with a gentleman who lived out in the wonderfully wooded forests of the Northwest. He was a potter. Perhaps the phrase "ceramic artist" is a better description. He was most certainly an artist, and I enjoyed watching his skill at spinning a pot and carving designs and firing his pots in his large kiln.

Years earlier he had served as an associate pastor in a

prominent church. But as sometimes happens, he had been terribly beaten up by the religious systems of his denomination. So he left organized religion, never to return. He didn't talk about it much, but the wounds were so deep that the idea of going into a church house was simply not an option for him. Even so, his faith in Jesus and his deep Christian spirituality was moving to me. As we would meet now and again out at his studio in the woods, I learned about sorrow and brokenness and grief. I also saw his light shine brightly; and I learned how a life could be re-shaped and re-formed into a thing of beauty, just like he did with the clay.

Now in this matter of the loss of a Christian consciousness, we who work in spiritual formation have a distinct advantage. You see, we are not focused on the modern ABCs of church success: Attendance, Buildings, and Cash. No. No. No. Our focus is on the growth of the soul. And this can be done anywhere and under any circumstance. Indeed, it is best done smack in the middle of the trials and tribulations of ordinary life.

3. Living Courageously through Dark Times

Now I am hesitant to speak with you about this third issue simply because it contains some hard words for us to hear and you might end up hearing nothing else I say. I hope this will not be the case. What is this third issue?

I believe an important pastoral task in the years to come will be for us to prepare our people to live courageously through dark times. Friends, we live in a wilderness of cultural unbelief. Our society in general now sees evangelicals as hypocrites who have surrendered their moral authority to the social and political currents of the times. And sadly, friends, we too often deserve the critique, and we need to repent of our complicity in the power structures of our day. We may even be witnessing the emergence of a new dark age. So we need to teach our people to sing the Lord's song in a strange land.

Now I know this may sound a bit like rhetorical exaggeration to some of you . . .

But if you are able to speak heart to heart with women who have been sexually abused and misused, then you understand what I mean.

If the teenagers in your youth group feel free to share with you their fear of being shot while at their high school, then you understand what I mean.

If your church contains immigrant people who live in constant fear of having their children taken from them, then you understand what I mean.

If you know African-American parents who are petrified that their children will be shot when they walk out the front door, then you understand what I mean.

I am saddened to say these things. I wish I could speak instead about sweetness and light and how a great new revival is just around the corner. But I cannot. And *we* should not. If we are to speak truth to power, we need to stand with Jeremiah of old, who rightly diagnosed the distorted language of his people, who were saying "'Peace, peace,' when there is no peace" (Jer 6:14). And today the fear-based narratives of racism and xenophobia, protectionism and white supremacy, have permeated the very fabric of American society. This, friends, is not the way of Jesus Christ.

Because we care deeply about genuine spiritual formation in ourselves and in our people and in our cultural landscape, we need to ask: Is there anything we can do about the moral squalor that abounds today? Oh yes, a great deal!

If we really want to be a countercultural people, I suggest first of all that we simply "shut up and listen." We listen to our neighbor. We listen to the angry. We listen to the fearful. We listen to the bruised and the broken. We listen, simply listen.

Next, we wait. Patiently. In faith. In hope. All the while we hold forth a flickering but inextinguishable light in the midst of the approaching darkness. We hold tightly to the promised word of the prophet Isaiah: "The people who walked in darkness have seen a great light" (Isa 9:2). Oh friends, how we need to recapture the good news of the evangel, which brings light to overcome darkness, hope to transform despair, and peace to conquer the violence of this emerging age.

Third, our listening and our waiting leads us to show forth a unique and countercultural way of living and speaking . . .

where justice and mercy are extended to all peoples;

where prayerful civility conquers angry rhetoric;

where compassion reaches out to the poor, the destitute, the hungry;

where plain, honest speech overcomes deceit and duplicity;

where gentleness, generosity, empathy, and kindness

govern our lives, our neighborhoods, and our nations; and where love reigns over all.

4. Narcissism Is the Spirit of the Age

Finally, I would like us to consider an issue that is particularly unique to our day in a way that simply was not the case forty years ago. In the contemporary scene today, *narcissism is the spirit of the age.* I wish I could say it more gently, but there it is. It is in the very air we breathe . . .

this extreme self-centeredness;

this total self-absorption;

this exaggerated sense of entitlement;

this utter self-obsession.

As you know, the word *narcissism* comes from Greek mythology, where Narcissus fell in love with his own image reflected in a pool of water. And today our selfie-obsessed, celebrity-driven culture has taken the vanity of Narcissus to the nth degree.

Friends, narcissism has no place in pastoral ministry. We simply must knock the spirit of narcissism in the head if we expect to mirror the example of Jesus—Jesus who "emptied himself" and became a person of no reputation (Phil 2:7). In this passage, the wise apostle Paul adds, "Do nothing from selfish ambition or conceit, but in humility regard others as better than yourselves. Let each of you look not to your own interests, but to the interests of others" (Phil 2:3-4).

In Colossians, Paul is even more emphatic: "Put to death, therefore, whatever in you is earthly: fornication, impurity, passion, evil desire, and greed (which is idolatry) . . . anger, wrath, malice, slander, and abusive language" (Col 3:5, 8).

The devotional masters had a wonderful recipe for dealing with the spirit of narcissism. It is captured in a double phrase that at first glance seems like a contradiction in terms, but upon careful examination we discover how very powerful the two components work together to deliver us from our narcissistic hankerings. The double phrase is *contemptus mundi* and *amor mundi*: "contempt for the world" and "love for the world."

It starts with *contemptus mundi*—our being torn loose from all earthly attachments and ambitions. This, in God's time and in God's way, will lead us into *amor mundi*—our being quickened to a divine but painful compassion for the world.

In the beginning, God plucks the world out of our hearts— *contemptus mundi*. Here we experience a loosening of the chains of attachment to positions of prominence and power. All our longing for social recognition is crucified. The desire to have our name in lights begins to appear puny and trifling. Slowly, ever so slowly, we begin to let go of all manipulative control, all human power plays, all managing of situations to make us look good. Freely and joyfully, we begin living without guile. A glorious detachment from all that this world offers overtakes our mind and heart and spirit. *Contemptus mundi.*

Then, just when we have become free from it all, God hurls the world back into our hearts—*amor mundi*—where

God and we together carry the world in infinitely tender love. We deepen in our compassion for the bruised, the broken, the dispossessed. We ache for and pray for and labor for others in a new way, a selfless way, a joy-filled way. Our heart is enlarged toward those on the margins: the orphan, the widow, the sojourner, the refugee. Indeed, our heart is enlarged toward all people, toward all of creation.

It was this reality, this *amor mundi*, that hurled St. Patrick back to Ireland to be the answer to its grinding spiritual poverty.

It was *amor mundi* that thrust Francis of Assisi into his worldwide ministry of compassion for the leper—indeed, for all people, all animals, all creation.

It was *amor mundi* that drove Elizabeth Fry into the hellhole of Newgate Prison, which led to her great work of prison reform.

It was *amor mundi* that caused William Wilberforce to labor his entire life for the abolition of the evil slave trade.

It was *amor mundi* that compelled William and Catherine Booth to serve tirelessly among the homeless of London, which led to the founding of the Salvation Army.

It was *amor mundi* that sent Father Damien to live and suffer and die among the lepers of the Hawaiian island of Molokai.

It was *amor mundi* that propelled Mother Teresa to minister among the poorest of the poor in India and throughout the world.

And it is *amor mundi* that compels millions of

ordinary folk like you and me to minister life in Christ's good name to our neighbor—our "nigh-bor," the person who is near us.

Let me share with you a wonderful experience that happened to Frank Laubach on the island of Mindanao in the Philippines in the 1930s. While on Mindanao, in experience after experience, God killed in Laubach all his sense of privilege and status and racial superiority—*contemptus mundi*. Then God gave him a prayer experiment that taught him to embrace the whole world—*amor mundi*. Listen to Laubach's own words:

This afternoon has brought a wonderful experience. I closed my eyes to pray and I saw the faces of those before me,
. . . then those in the houses nearby,
. . . then those down the line, and across the river,
. . . and down the highway in the next town,
. . . and the next, and the next,
. . . then in concentric circles around the lake, and over the mountains to the coast,
. . . then across the sea to the north,
. . . then over the wide ocean to California,
. . . then across America to the people whom I know,
. . . then over to Europe to the people whom I have met there,
. . . then to the Near East where my missionary friends live,
. . . then to India where I have other friends,

. . . to others in China,

. . . and to the multitudes who are suffering the dreadful pangs of cold and starvation—around the world in less than a minute, and for a time the whole of my soul seemed to be lit up with a divine light as it held the world up to God!

Amor mundi.

Let's pray . . .

O Lord, whose life and light and power is over all, would you touch the deepest chambers of our heart:
> *molding,*
>> *shaping,*
>>> *forming,*
>>>> *transforming.*

May we enter the compassion of Jesus on every level of daily experience. Loving Lord, please . . .
> *purify our spirit,*
>> *renew our mind,*
>>> *sanctify our imagination, and*
>>>> *enlarge our soul.*

Thank you! Thank you! Thank you!

—Amen.

Printed in the USA
CPSIA information can be obtained
at www.ICGtesting.com
LVHW010359081224
798606LV00005B/1205